John Elway

Presented by
Beckett Publications

John Elway

Published by: Beckett Publications

15850 Dallas Parkway

Dallas, TX 75248

ISBN: 1-887432-74-4

First Edition: January 1999

Beckett Corporate Sales and Information

(972) 991-6657

Foreword

By Tracy Hackler

There's a look that invades John Elway's eyes — an eerie, possessed trance — when he's about to make NFL history. Surely you've noticed it before.

Perhaps you witnessed it in 1983, when the embattled rookie shocked Baltimore with three fourth-quarter scoring strikes, the first of the now-legendary 40-plus acts of fourth-quarter heroism.

Maybe you fell under his spell in 1987, when John Elway became just "Elway" in the closing moments of the AFC Championship Game in frozen Cleveland Stadium. In what would become known as simply "The Drive," Elway staged a 15-play, 98-yard ascension to superstardom. Instant replay will never let us forget the famous game-tying touchdown dart to Mark Jackson that no doubt left the "Elway Cross" and provided the impetus for Denver's 23-20 overtime win and the first of three painful Super Bowl defeats for Elway and Company.

The world noticed the look again last January, a full 11 years later, when Elway departed the pocket late in the third quarter of Super Bowl XXXII and embarked on the most consequential eight-yard gain in Super Bowl history. He hurled himself headfirst into a three-man Green Bay gang, a wall of violent resistance that sent the 37-year-old mass of hyper-competitive spirit helicoptering harshly to the Qualcomm Stadium grass. The immediate result, of course, was a first down; the ultimate result was, well, the ultimate result.

The Broncos won that game, 31-24, punctuating a career that was worthy of a book long before, but only then became a complete literary work because of the fitting ending.

The people in Elway's life — the ones for whom he's made careers and ruined careers, and the ones who have helped make his career — know better than anyone where he ranks in the grand scheme of NFL history.

Terrell Davis knows. Dan Reeves knows. Brett Favre knows. Mike Shanahan knows. They've seen The Drive. They've seen The Dive. They've seen The Look. It's fitting then, that through their eyes, you see this book.

Tracy Hackler, editor of Beckett Football Card Monthly *for three years, is now a senior editor at Beckett Publications.*

Contents

Air Force

"I think John is the best to ever play the game. . . . I think he's the greatest quarterback ever."

John always has had fire. As I've said so many times, he's the ultimate competitor. If you're playing pingpong, he's gonna play it like it's the Super Bowl. If you're playing cards, he's gonna play like everything's on the line. He's always got this deep, burning desire to win. We have that in common. That was one of the first things that drew us together.

I came to the Broncos before John's second year. His rookie year had been tough for him. Right away, we started lifting weights together, and that's how our relationship started. I got to know him, and he got to know me. We had a lot of fun lifting together.

As a position coach, you always go through a lot of things with a quarterback, and over the years, John and I have gone through a lot together. There's a bond there, a trust there, and most of all, there's a belief in each other.

With Shanahan as the new receivers coach and Elway settled in at starter, it was far from mere coincidence that the Broncos rolled to a 13-3 record in 1984.

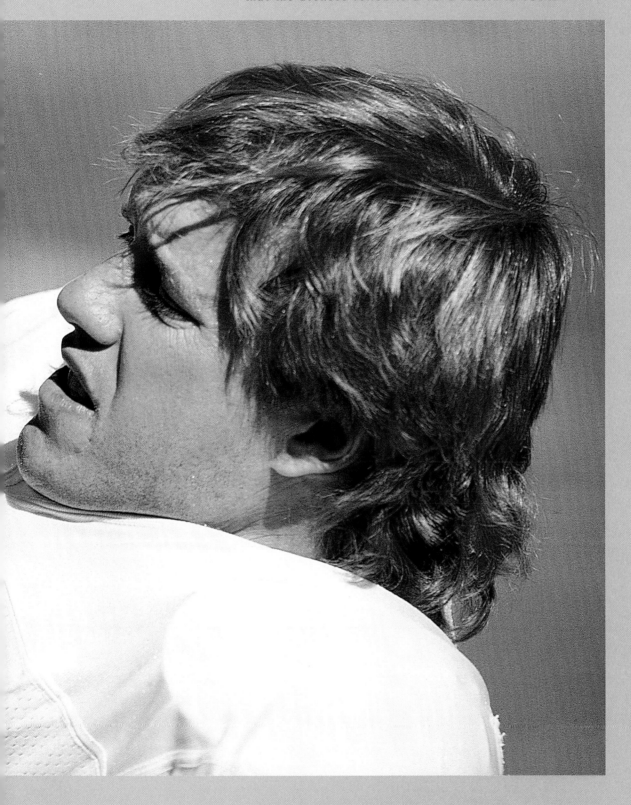

As offensive coordinator from 1985 to 1987, Shanahan
watched his quarterback direct 12 game-winning or
game-saving drives in the fourth quarter.

It helps so much when a player knows — really knows — you care for him. You've been through the wars together. He knows how you react under pressure. He knows that when the going gets tough, you're going to be there and not going to turn away.

The Drive against Cleveland (in the 1986 AFC Championship Game) was obviously one of John's great moments. Before that victory, I think John, like a lot of quarterbacks, got stereotyped. He didn't go to a bowl game at Stanford, and in the NFL we had yet to win a championship or go to the Super Bowl. So it was great for him to be able to win that game, especially in that environment and situation in Cleveland. John deserved so much credit because he almost single-handedly got us through the playoffs. All his skills came together on that drive.

John can beat you in so many different ways. He can kill you with one deep pass. He can get you by scrambling or running for a long gain after you think you've got him for a loss. And he can beat you with a ball-possession offense that takes advantage of his own running, short passing and leadership. And he basically did all that on The Drive.

In fact, John basically carried us through three playoff games and into the Super Bowl (against the Giants in XXI). That's such a credit to him and the fact he was able to make plays when nothing was there.

If John had come out of his rookie year with the type of players and the system we have now, I think he'd have a number of Super Bowl wins under his belt. I don't think there's any record he wouldn't own. When

I was with John for the three Super Bowl losses, I made tapes of those games and took them to clinics. I'd try to explain what we were doing on offense, but most of the plays were just John freewheeling and making something happen when everything broke down.

There's probably been less pressure on John the last couple years than ever before, because of Terrell Davis and other people. John's been having fun because he's playing at such a high level. He's been truly exceptional.

From 1986 to 1996, Elway made seven trips to the Pro Bowl, claimed an NFL MVP award and helped Denver win three AFC championships.

18 |

John always told me, "The most important thing is that I want to make sure I'm playing at a high level. If I feel like my game is going downhill, I don't want to be hanging around."

He also wants to enjoy the game. And he's been doing that. He's played the game as well as I've seen him play it. He's throwing the ball extremely well. He's at the peak.

The diving play in the Super Bowl against Green Bay, the one near the end zone, well, I've seen him make plays like that all along. Not very many people ever see a guy 37 years old make a play like that. It picked up the whole

The pain of three losses in the Super Bowl made the victory over Green Bay in XXXII that much sweeter for the head coach and his quarterback.

sideline. When your quarterback does something like that, it just transfers to the whole team. I don't know if I felt, "We have it," when he did that, but it sure fired up the team. It's that kind of leadership — leadership by action — that makes such a difference.

To think of him or any quarterback throwing for more than 50,000 yards is unbelievable. Just to think about what you have to go through to reach that record is unbelievable. It takes a lot of years doing a great job to get to that point. But John is such a team guy. I don't think he'll really enjoy it until he's done playing.

To be a good coach, you have to have great players, and to be a great team, you need a great quarterback. John Elway has obviously been great for my career and has played a huge role in helping me to come to the point where I am now.

I've already said it: I think John is the best to ever play the game. I guess other people will decide that. But I think he's the greatest quarterback ever.

Since John Elway's 1983 debut in Denver, Mike Shanahan has served more than 10 years with the Broncos in four different stints. He joined the staff in '84 as receivers coach, then worked closely with Elway as quarterbacks coach and offensive coordinator before becoming head coach in 1995.

"We make a real good team out on the field. Defenses still fear him, obviously."

By Terrell Davis

As told to Clay Latimer

I was really intimidated the first time I lined up with John Elway. I had butterflies because I had never really practiced with John until I started that first week against Buffalo in my rookie season. And you know, when you're growing up, playing with neighborhood kids, someone's always pretending to be John Elway.

In training camp, John would practice once a day, and only with the first team. I was fourth and fifth on the depth chart. So I only took handoffs from Bill Musgrave and Hugh Millen. But before the Buffalo game, I finally took my first handoff from John. When I came back to the huddle I could hear John telling (offensive coordinator) Gary Kubiak to tell me to open up my hands a little wider to give him a bigger pocket. I'm thinking, "Oh man, I'm messing up already. I can't get the big man upset."

With 1,117 yards in his rookie season, it didn't take Terrell Davis long to prove that his rushing was the perfect complement to Elway's passing.

A quarterback is the leader. You go out there and you want to try to gain his confidence and respect. If you make a mistake, you might say, "Oh my goodness, he's not going to have confidence in me. He's not going to give me the ball or throw a pass to me." Or you're afraid he could go to the coaches and tell them, "I don't want this kid in the huddle." John Elway has the pull to do that. But he never did. Every once in a while, if you're walking back to the huddle, or if you're carrying your butt back to the huddle, or if you drop a pass, he'll say, "Come on, T.D." Something like that.

One of my biggest moments came early, when John Elway said to the media that I was the best running back he's ever played with in Denver. To have somebody like John say that about a back like me, especially at that time in my career when I'd just come into the league, well, that was a super confidence booster. You couldn't ask for anything more than that.

John has gone out of his way to help me. This offense is kind of complicated. In fact, it's very complicated, and each week we're doing something different. So a lot of times, if I don't know what I'm doing, I'm going to ask John. But a lot of times he can just sense that. Almost from the first day, we've been able to communicate non-verbally. But once again, I think the thing that John did — the very best thing he did for me — was not saying anything negative about me. That was crucial.

We make a real good team out on the field. Defenses still fear him, obviously. And they probably fear me. I see our combination resembling Emmitt Smith and Troy Aikman. Right now John Elway has something that he never really had, and

After Davis took his first ever handoff in practice from the future Hall of Famer, Elway could be heard telling an assistant coach to instruct T.D. to open his hands wider to give the QB a larger target. Davis, like any smart rookie, took the advice.

that's a complete package on offense. He has great wide receivers. He has a good running game. For once in his career he feels like he can go out there and play a game and not feel that he has to carry the whole team for the bulk of the game.

People say, "This is your team, Terrell." That never bothered him. From what I hear, even John said that. But we all know what John can do. Take the Super Bowl (against Green Bay), for example, and that diving run. I'm in the pocket. I see him leave the pocket and I'm looking because it's third down, and he just takes off running. I'm thinking he's going to slide. He's still running as people are getting closer and closer to him, and the next thing you know he jumps up in the air, gets hit, does some little flips, falls down, and we have the first down. Right

Davis, the lowest-drafted rookie to rush for 1,000 yards, helped Elway's fans live out their Super Bowl dreams.

then and there I knew we were going to win that game. I got up and said, "Man, if this guy can do this. . . ." John was giving up his body for the team to win this game. We couldn't do any less.

John and I couldn't really talk right after the game. I mean, after the Super Bowl it's wild. But later we hung out and I told him I was happy for him, and he said he was happy for me. Obviously, it's a very good feeling to say I helped the greatest quarterback of all time win a championship. Everybody would've respected his deci-

sion to retire after the Super Bowl win. Everybody I talked to wanted him back, but they said, "If I'm John, I'm not coming back."

It was kind of hard waiting for his decision because I didn't know what he was thinking. Sometimes you couldn't help but think, "What if he doesn't come back?" I was trying to convince myself that if he didn't come back we were going to be OK. But it was kind of hard to imagine. I didn't want to see the unknown. I'm not ready for that yet. He's helped my career tremendously. He's the only quarterback I've ever played with.

So when I heard on the news that he was coming back, I was happy. All day I was just driving around saying, "Man, John's coming back." He's taken a lot off pressure off me. He's the leader — no doubt.

Every time you get in the huddle with John, it's an amazing experience. Each day you're out there, you have to respect and admire him and be thankful that you can play one more game with him. And then another game. And one after that. I'm happy I've even had the opportunity to play with him. Originally, I was hoping to do it for one year. Now I'm in my fourth year.

These are great days for me.

Nearing the midway point of the 1998 season, Terrell Davis came up with a 136-yard performance against Jacksonville to become just the third running back in NFL history to break the 1,000-yard barrier by the seventh game of the year. The other two are Eric Dickerson and Jim Brown.

"I've never seen anything like John's arm. I heard how he cut one receiver's finger to the bone."

By Ed McCaffrey

As told to Clay Latimer

John Elway's arm is relatively small, so how does he get all that power? I wish I knew.

You see pitchers in baseball and some of them have pretty bad bodies, and you're wondering how in the world they can throw the ball 100 miles per hour, and I have no idea. But a lot of it is just rhythm, and obviously strength, coordination and natural ability.

I've never seen anything like John's arm. I heard all about it when I went to Stanford. Stories about his arm were part of the lore. I heard how he cut one receiver's finger to the bone. I heard about the Elway Cross, the "X" mark his ball leaves when it hits you in the chest. I've gotten the Elway Cross. I've had the wind knocked out of me. It's not a good feeling.

By the time Ed McCaffrey got to Stanford, stories of the "Elway Cross" had reached near-legendary status.

He basically broke my finger in training camp (before the 1998 season). I ran a slant route and he just fired it in there and caught my finger wrong and snapped it like it was nothing. I was maybe 25 or 30 yards away from him. Whenever you can throw hard enough to break a finger, you know he's putting some heat behind the ball.

You have to be ready at all times. It's strictly reaction. The ball is coming. You kind of see a brown dot coming at you at light speed and you just stick your hands where you think the ball is.

I don't want to make it sound like John throws every ball that way. He doesn't. But when it's a tight squeeze and the defensive back is close to you and John has a small window, he has the ability to fire it in there and at least give you an opportunity to make a catch.

McCaffrey had 103 catches before he came to Denver,
but he was still left in awe of Elway's arm strength.

There's one thing John does that I've never personally seen
another quarterback do: He can wait for a receiver to come out of
his break, make sure that he's out of his break safely, and then
throw the ball. You have to have a cannon to be able to do that.

Most quarterbacks rely on timing, and there's a little bit of timing to it with John. But a lot of times, he can eliminate the timing aspect by waiting for you to get open before throwing. He has enough arm strength to get it to you before the defensive back can react, and that's a unique ability. That's something I definitely wasn't used to until I came here.

It's shocking how far John can throw the ball. During my first year here (1995), I wasn't used to playing with quarterbacks with that sort of arm strength. I ran a "go" route and probably started throttling it down after 60 yards because the play broke down. I was thinking the play was over and he overthrew me by about 10 yards. I'd started running again, so the ball had to land 80 yards down the field. This was in a practice. I

One of Elway's many attributes is his field vision, which helped him send eight TD passes to McCaffrey in 1997.

couldn't believe it.

I didn't play with him when he was 23, but I'm guessing that he could've thrown the ball end zone to end zone. I mean, he can throw it a good 80 yards now.

John's famous for the play where he runs to the right, stops, pivots and then throws the ball 40 yards down the field and 30 yards across. That's a 70-yard pass. To do that — and to get it there before the defense reacts — is very, very difficult. Often times, John's at his best when a play breaks down because he can throw so well on the run.

When you combine his athleticism — his instincts, the way he sees the field — with his arm strength, well, he's really effective.

Our feeling is that the play is never over as long as

John has the ball. You could be the length of the field away and somehow he's going to find a way to get it to you. In fact, you're overcome by a feeling of urgency to get open, because he can get the ball to you. You just keep working as hard as you can and something happens.

He can see you from anywhere. He can get the ball to you from anywhere. It's so hard for the defense because he's able to run at full speed, dodge tackles and still look upfield. It's kind of like being able to dribble full speed along the court without looking at the ball.

I don't think he zeros in on one receiver, either. I think that's a mistake a lot of quarterbacks probably make. He looks at the whole field and waits for something to happen, and he can anticipate when a guy is going to get open. That's a tough skill to master.

But what makes John special is his touch. He has one of the strongest arms in the league, and you have to be able to throw it hard. But there are a lot of guys with real strong arms who never make it in the NFL, and that's because it takes touch to play in this league. You also have to be able to drop it over the defender or time-up with your receiver. He has the ability to do both, and that's what has made him such a great quarterback.

His arm is just a natural gift. I don't know if it's something you can coach or something you're just born with. It's hard to figure.

After catching on with the New York Giants to the tune of 92 receptions in his first three NFL seasons, Ed McCaffrey spent a year with the 49ers before really finding a home in Denver. Of the first 33 touchdown receptions of his career, John Elway had thrown 21 of them.

4

Baptism by Fire

"He was the best-looking rookie I've ever seen. I expected him to go out and perform miracles."

Until John Elway's rookie year, I'd always believed in the basic philosophy that it took three to five years before a quarterback could play.

But John had such a good preseason (in 1983) that I really felt he was ready. I actually thought he wouldn't have any problems and that we could get better as the season went along. He was awesome in the preseason. He hit like, I don't know what it was, 60-something percent of his passes. He was the best-looking rookie I've ever seen. With so much talent in one individual, I expected him to go out and perform miracles.

With that early success, I might have been under a lot of pressure if I hadn't started him. I talked to John, and he was a little bit amazed when I told him he was going to start. He was so excited. He may have had an idea that he wasn't ready, but he never would have said that. He was

Elway started the first five games of his rookie season, was benched in favor of Steve DeBerg, then came back with a vengeance the last five games when DeBerg was injured.

such a competitive person. He was going to do whatever I asked him to do.

Still, it was unfair on my part. The mistake I made — the biggest mistake — was not realizing the difference between the preseason and the regular season. Nobody plays as hard in preseason as they do in the regular season. Teams threw everything at John, and I couldn't help him. I realized later how much was involved in starting a rookie quarterback.

John had never been in a situation where he had to scrape to do well. And I think John wanted too badly for the other players on the team to accept him. I should have made Steve DeBerg the starter. After five preseason games, they were about even, but I made my decision.

Five NCAA records meant nothing to NFL defenders, who greeted a wide-eyed Elway with much hostility in 1983. Elway was rated 17th among AFC passers that year.

John was smart. He knew what he was doing out there, but it was processed knowledge. It was studied knowledge. He could pass the test on being a quarterback, but the game itself was different. It was a struggle for him to get the play called in the huddle, get up to the line of scrimmage, and get the play off before the 45-second clock expired. My misjudgment could have really damaged him, but he was such a strong, confident person that it didn't hurt him that much. It may have set him back, but he overcame poor coaching.

The first game was in Pittsburgh and, defensively, they threw all kinds of things at him. Then we played in Baltimore the next week. The Colts, of course, had taken John with the first pick of the draft, but John said he wouldn't play for them. I expected something, but I had no idea the reaction would be the way it was. Every time he walked on the field, he was booed.

After being the most hyped college passer in nearly two decades, Elway was drafted by the Colts before being traded to Denver.

It was unmerciful. I don't think there's ever been a situation like that, and to this day, I don't know if he was bruised by that game.

I can remember the first play of the game. For the first pass, I was trying to give him something that would be an easy completion to kind of settle him down a little bit. I remember he must have thrown it about 40 yards

Unlike Elway, Brian Griese, a rookie quarterback in 1998, is being brought along slowly by the Broncos.

on a dead line. It never got more than shoulder high. If somebody had caught it, it probably would have driven a hole in him. He was wired, definitely.

You know, looking back, maybe the best thing for him was that he was benched for four or five weeks, and he could study at his own pace. He worked hard during that time. And there was a tremendous difference in him when he came back. He was better able to digest the system. He was so much more comfortable with what we were doing.

When he came back, he was ready. He was unbelievable in a comeback victory over Baltimore. I think it was the first NFL game his dad had seen him play in person. We were down 19-0 and he led us all the way back.

The progress he made from the first game against Baltimore to the second was remarkable. It did so much for our defense, our offense, for

everybody. Everyone said, "Hey, golly, we can win when it looks like the game is over."

I've watched film of Peyton Manning in both games (in 1998) against New England. And the difference in him from the first game to the second game was incredible. You see the same type of improvement in Manning that you saw in John from the first to the second Baltimore game.

John made his biggest improvement from his first to his second year. He was so much more comfortable with everything. It is sort of like a guy studying Spanish: He could pass the course, but if he went to Mexico, he wouldn't even understand what people were saying. Well, by his second year, John could do more than just pass the test.

John's had an amazing career. To be playing 15 years later, let alone this well, is really amazing. Since we didn't always have the greatest offensive line for him, he took a tremendous amount of hits, got sacked and everything.

He came to a team that wasn't at the bottom of the standings, a team drafting most of the time in the late 20s. Plus, there wasn't free agency then. We just couldn't go out and get players that we needed or wanted. But he hung in there.

Dan Reeves teamed with John Elway to lead the Broncos to 98 regular season victories and three Super Bowl appearances in 10 seasons in Denver. Reeves left Denver after the '92 season and promptly won a combined 20 games in his first two seasons with the New York Giants before joining the Atlanta Falcons prior to the 1997 season.

Mirror Image

5

"I always felt like I played like him, and after I met him, I felt like I was like him off the field."

My first memories of John Elway go back to when I was in junior high. I remember him coming out of college and going to Baltimore in the draft and then getting traded to Denver. Once I started watching him play in the NFL, I liked him because I felt like I played the same way he played even when I was that age. I ran around, had a strong arm, and I could make some things happen.

The first time I played against him was in 1993 in a Sunday night game at Lambeau Field. It was an honor to play against him. I wanted to beat him more than the team itself, and I wanted to outplay him. I was thinking, "Here's the chance of a lifetime. Here's the guy who, when I was a kid, I watched play. Here's a chance to shine." I remember it clearly. We won that game.

I'm not sure when I first met John and actually spent some time

In 1997, 37-year-old John Elway and 29-year-old Brett Favre had remarkably similar seasons: Elway completed 55.8 percent of his passes, Favre 59.3; Elway had an 87.5 rating, Favre a 92.6.

talking to him. But I remember I was in awe. It seemed like he took me under his wing from the start. We all went out, a bunch of quarterbacks, and I remember thinking, "This is pretty cool. You get to hang out with your idol."

Now I know him real well. I consider us good friends. The thing about it is, I always felt like I played like him, and once I got the chance to meet him, I felt like I was like him even off the field. We've never let the success go to our heads, and we appreciate the jobs we have. We respect it. When you watch us play, you see that. When you watch him, even at his age, he's still having fun. That's why he's still playing.

I'm the same exact way. We're fortunate enough to make a lot of money and be in the spotlight and have all the focus on us. But we try not to let it go to our heads. We're not fancy on or off the field. We like golf and we do things for charities. Everything he does, I do, and it's not because I saw what he did and said, "That's what I'm going to do." I just kind of

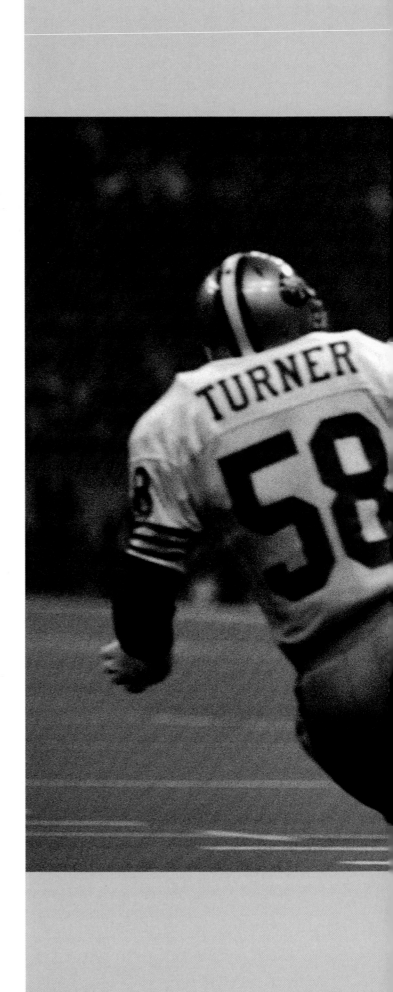

Both Favre and Elway weren't afraid to run for their
lives early in their careers. Favre rushed for 216 yards
his third season; Elway ran for 253 in his third season.

happened to evolve into the same thing he is.

I see him at the Quarterback Challenge every year and we play in a couple of golf tournaments together each year. We did a commercial for the NFL together last year. We end up seeing each other four or five times a year. I call him occasionally just to talk and see how his wife, Janet, and the kids are doing. His son, Jack . . . well, as John says, "If it wasn't for me, you'd be his favorite player."

We went to Disney World together, my wife, Deanna, and I and our daughter, Brittany, along with John and his family. We kind of hung out, and Jack was hanging around me. It was funny because it seemed like Jack was a little nervous — at least that's what John said — but I

An optimistic Brett Favre expressed his utmost respect for John Elway as he prepared to play against his hero.

Few quarterbacks play the game like Elway and Favre: always hard, always tough, and always with enthusiasm.

was hitting him and asking, "Hey, how you doin'?" He was a little nervous, and I was like, "Who's your dad? He's one of the most famous players ever."

You've got to have fun in this game, and when you watch John play, you see him having fun. People enjoy that. Too many times the bad things are brought out — the money we make, all the attention we get — but to see guys treating it like they were back in the fifth grade, it's fun to watch. That's what it's all about.

Of course, the one time when we met professionally with everything on the line was at the Super Bowl. On that day I didn't care who I was playing against, I wanted to win the game. It could have been my brother across from me and I would have wanted to win as badly as I did the year before. But after it was over, as bad as I felt, I felt good for John. It's nice that he won one after losing three times.

I went up to him after the game and I obviously felt bad, and I said, "Great job, I'm happy for you," and all that. And it wasn't a front. He knew that, but I'm sure he could see my disappointment. He said, "You know what? I know you feel bad and everything, but imagine what I've been through to get where I am right now. You did it last year in your first Super Bowl." I said, "You're right, not that at this moment it makes me feel any better."

But in a way it did make me feel better. Not only is it an honor to play in the Super Bowl, but I won in my first try. There he was in his 15th year still trying to win one. Of all the things he accomplished, that's the one thing that had slipped through until then. I did feel better talking to him.

Through all that time, he really has been a special player. When he plays, anything can happen. He doesn't play careful, he plays to win. You look at quarterbacks who do play careful, and then you see him make plays that other quarterbacks wouldn't attempt. I'm the same way.

Sure it's gotten us in trouble, but would I trade the way I play for those five or six bad plays a year? No. And he wouldn't, either. That's what makes him special. You see him dive, you see him block. Other guys do that too, but we take it to the next level. He's got a strong arm, he's smart, he can avoid pass rushers and all that. But so what? Other guys can do that. He's willing to take the risks that other quarterbacks aren't willing to take.

Nowadays, he probably has to play a little more careful. Not that he wants to, but he has missed some games with injuries. He knows if he goes out and plays the way I would play today, he probably wouldn't be around at the end of the season. They have too good a team for him to risk injury at this point. He's playing smarter now, and I think he has to. Steve Young does it, too. Older quarterbacks have to do it.

But John still has that great arm. People sometimes ask who's got the better arm between us, and I'd say I do now. But it would have been interesting to see who had the strongest arm when we were both 25 years old. I'm sure he was a faster runner. He's definitely got more rushing yards than I could ever dream of.

Brett Favre was 13 years old when John Elway made his NFL debut. Thirteen years later, one year after leading the Packers to a world title, Favre lost to his friend, 31-24, in Super Bowl XXXII.

Worst Nightmare

6

"His mobility is what really sets him apart. It's what makes him such a nightmare to defend against."

When I came to the Broncos after all those years in Kansas City, John told me, "Welcome to the good side. I'm glad to get you off my back." That felt really good to be welcomed with open arms. And it felt good because it's so hard to play against him.

What's it like to play against him? Don't remind me. One game we were up by 21 points, or something like that, and he scored 21 points in two minutes. It was ridiculous. That was the game he threw this unbelievable pass. He ran to the right side, stopped, and threw it like 60 yards all the way to the left side. The receiver was standing all the way on the other side waiting to catch it like it was a fair catch. It's one of

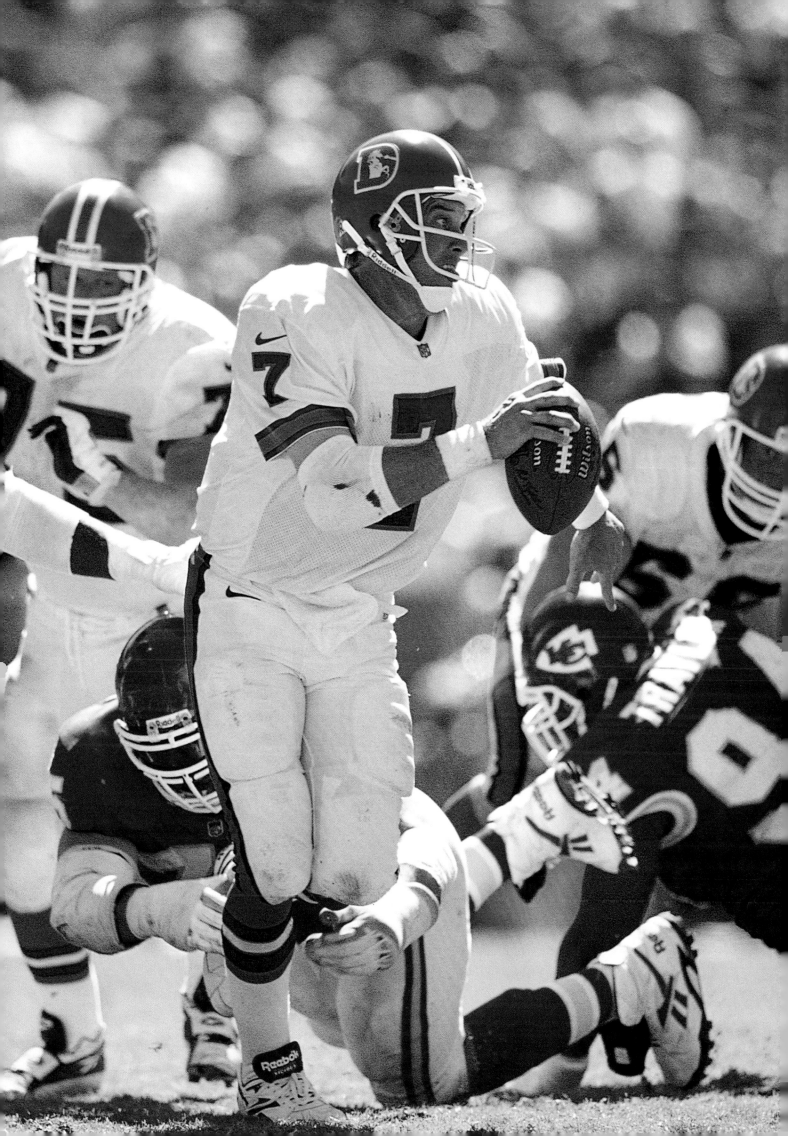

Neil Smith knows first hand how elusive Elway can be.
During his nine years in Kansas City, he registered 15
sacks against Denver, but remembers all too well the
many times the quarterback got away.

the most lethal plays I've seen him make.

His mobility is what really sets him apart. It's what makes him such a nightmare to defend against. I mean, his arm is so deadly. The thing is, he does so much damage when he scrambles. You think you've got him stopped, cornered or whatever. Then, all of a sudden, he's not only loose, he's running, and then he sees some receiver open way down the field. You just know he's going to get the ball to him no matter how far away the receiver is.

So everything can fall apart — just like that! He's so good at making you miss a tackle or sack. He can just feel you, even when you're behind him.

His football knowledge will always get you. You have to have smarts to be a good quarterback, and he definitely has smarts. He knows how to make reads and how to escape the rush. You have to have a good feel for every-thing if you're the quarterback, and he has a good feel for everything. I mean, he's the leader. He knows it all. And he was taught all that a long time ago.

You always fear Elway in the fourth quarter, especially at Mile High, because you're just sucking wind because of the altitude. You just dread it. But sometimes, Elway isn't even hurting you. Just the fear of him is what bugs you. Then he ends up hurting you.

I'll bet most of his comebacks came against (the Chiefs). He's got a great record against Marty Schottenheimer, and I don't think Marty will ever be able for forget it. First when he was head coach in Cleveland, then in Kansas City. I'm sure Marty has nightmares about (Elway beating him).

I had the most sacks against John, and it's probably because he took me to another level when I played against him. I knew he could eat us alive back there, and I was young and hungry. I could run a little bit, too.

But after you'd sack him, really crush him, he'd just get up and grin at you with those big ol' teeth, man. It was like he was saying, "Yeah, you didn't hurt me. Wait 'til the next play." And then he'd come back and throw a touchdown on you. That hurt.

I feel really comfortable now when Elway's in the game. Now that he's on my side I can cross my legs and sit back and relax. Since I've been here he hasn't gotten into one of those comebacks where he's racing up and down the field. But he can still do it. The good thing now is that he has help.

John is a great competitor. He plays hurt. He'll risk everything to win. Against Oakland (in Week 12 of the

Elway's career is full of dramatic games against Marty Schottenheimer, whether the coach was with the Chiefs or the Cleveland Browns. Elway threw for 385 yards against Cleveland in the 1989 AFC Championship Game.

1998 season) we threw a pass to him. Even though he had problems the week or two before with sore ribs, he just went for it (and made the reception). That's something for some 38-year-old guy to do. Other players see that and say, "If Elway can go for it like that, I better too." Things like that are pretty inspiring, like the play in the Super Bowl. What can you say after a play like that?

When he dived into those Packers players during the Super Bowl you could see all his desire to win. When I see replays in slow motion, the first thing I see are his eyes.

Elway has been sacked more than 500 times in his career, resulting in losses of more than 3,700 yards. But sacks don't count against a quarterback's rushing total, leaving Elway in the top five in all-time rushing yards for a quarterback with 3,313 entering the 1998 season.

You can see it in his eyes that he knew we had to get the first down. He laid his body on the line for the game, and it made the difference. That play sums up his competitiveness.

It was something special when he broke the 50,000-yard mark for career passing against Oakland (in Week 12). That's a lot of real estate; that's a lot of mileage. After he did it, on the sideline, I said to him, "Could you ever run that distance?" He said, "Maybe if I start now I could get there before I die."

The biggest surprise in getting to know him is how real he is. Some people get caught up in all the fame, but he turned out to be real humble. He's good people. I saw the same thing in Joe Montana. As big as Joe was, he was always good to his teammates.

John Elway is No. 1 in my book. He doesn't act like a guy who's 38 years old. He still has the amazing arm, he can still move around, and he can still make recoveries from bad situations. I know, because I think he got a lot of those 50,000 yards against me.

All-Pro defensive end Neil Smith, who played nine seasons with the Kansas City Chiefs before signing with Denver in 1997, entered the 1998 season with 95 quarterback sacks, 15 of those at the expense of John Elway.

7

Heartbreaker

"Unfortunately, in those great games, he made a lot more big plays than we did."

I don't want to talk about John Elway. He's the reason I never played in a Super Bowl.

No, really, other than the obvious — he can throw the ball a mile and he can scramble — the thing about John Elway is, even if you do all the right things on defense, he can still do something to beat you. He's done it for so long we kind of take it for granted now.

I remember the first time we played against him, when he was a rookie in 1983. Of course, we also played against him when we had a chance to go to the Super Bowl in 1986, '87 and '89. The back-to-back AFC Championship games, as everyone knows, were great games, tremendously exciting for anyone who watched them. But from that first game against Elway until the last, he always seemed the same. He was always really quiet on the field. He never seemed to get upset.

Some quarterbacks complain a lot to the referees about anything that's even close to pass interference. But I don't remember him being that way at all. He's just a great competitor, a great athlete, and he'd never do or say anything that would upset the defense.

The impression I got was that he was a quality person. I never really saw him complain to a referee. If things didn't go well for him, I would never see any body language, or any other outward sign, that conveyed he was down on himself. He would just keep lining up and making plays.

I also never got the impression that he was rattled. He played the game like a kid, like a young kid. His enthusiasm showed more through his actions. When he had an opportunity to run, he'd just take off and run. With a lot of quarterbacks, when they run, you can almost see their body language saying, "I really don't want to be doing this, but I will." Elway ran with the enthusiasm of a running back. Steve Young does the same thing.

As a team in all those big games in the '80s, we felt that Elway was a better quarterback when things broke down and he had to scramble. It's kind of funny, but I think we felt that if he had to drop back — take the clas-

Some of Elway's biggest games have come in the postseason, such as the 302-yard performance in a '93 playoff game against the Raiders.

Elway and the Broncos ended the season of Marty Schottenheimer
and the Browns in the playoffs three times in the late '80s.

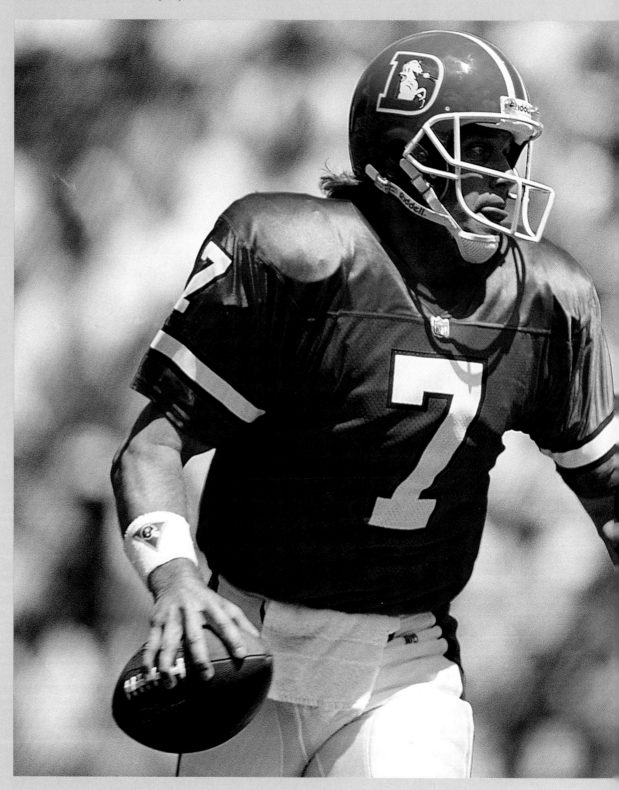

sic three- or five- or seven-step drop, read the defense, and then throw the ball — we didn't really feel he could beat us. But if he dropped back and something wasn't there, and then he took off — either to run or to scramble and then throw — he became the most dangerous player on the field.

Now, later in his career, I think he's changed. With the running attack they have now, I think he's willing to take what the defense gives him. And there's a lot more to give now, because people have to stop the run against Denver. He didn't have that early in his career. He was forced to try to create plays. Now, Denver pounds the ball in there, and eventually the defense has to put up some sort of stacked front to slow down the run. With the receivers they have, that gives them more opportunities downfield. He accepts that role now, and he makes the throws he needs to make.

Unfortunately, in those great games, he made a lot more big plays than we did. Everything he did, he did with an enthusiasm

In the loss to the Raiders, Elway had 23 of Denver's 56 rushing yards.

91

that was under the surface. It wasn't like he was pumping his fists or jumping up and down after a great play. By the way he played — the way he took his drops and the other mechanics that good quarterbacks must have — I got the impression that he felt he was always just one play away from making the play that could win the game for them.

As far as the rivalry between us, sure, we were disappointed to lose. But it was never like I hated losing to John Elway. I think we all felt that way because he had so much class. He never gave you anything to get upset at him with, other than the fact that he was such a heck of a player and so hard to beat.

Even in the 1986 AFC Championship Game in Cleveland, when Denver was down there backed up in the Dawg Pound and the fans were throwing all those batteries and dog biscuits at him, I don't remember him complaining. I don't remember him trying to put it back in the fans' faces. I only remember that it seemed like, when all that was happening, he was just thinking about what he was going to do on the next play. I think that's how much he was into the game.

When Denver beat us with The Drive in 1986, it might seem funny to say this, but I just remember one thing. We had them backed up way down there, and they kept moving it upfield and then he made that great throw (to Mark Jackson for the touchdown). That's all I really remember about it — the great throw he made at the end that finished off The Drive.

In a nutshell, that was the one thing about him. He had that passion for competing, for somehow finding a way to get it done when he had to get it done. For lack of a better word, there's a certain kind of buzz that comes over you when you're out there competing. I think he loved the feeling of running around, zipping the ball in there and playing the game wide open. If he didn't play that way, I don't know if he could have kept that drive going for 90-some yards or whatever it was.

When I look at Young and Brett Favre now, I see the same things I saw in Elway. He was quiet. He wasn't a smart aleck or anything. He never had problems with any other player on the field. I think those are some of the reasons that I really had a lot of respect for Elway.

Through the years, that's what impressed me the most. He came to compete every time. There are plenty of talented athletes in all sports, but they don't always come to play every time. With Elway, I think you could always count on him to give his best.

I don't know if I could ever put myself in the same class as an athlete with him, so maybe the best way for me to really describe how I felt about him is to say that he played quarterback like I would have liked to play it. Wide open. Throw it here. Run there. Scramble around and try to zip it in between two guys 40 yards downfield. I would have loved to be able to do that.

That's probably why he's played for so long. He has a real passion for playing the game the way it should be played.

Clay Matthews spent 16 seasons as a member of the Cleveland Browns linebacking corps, going to four Pro Bowls while registering a Browns-record 63.5 sacks. Three times he helped Cleveland to the AFC Championship Game, only to lose to Elway's Broncos each time.

Class Act

8

"When John won the Super Bowl, I couldn't have been happier, finally getting the monkey off the backs of the quarterback class of '83."

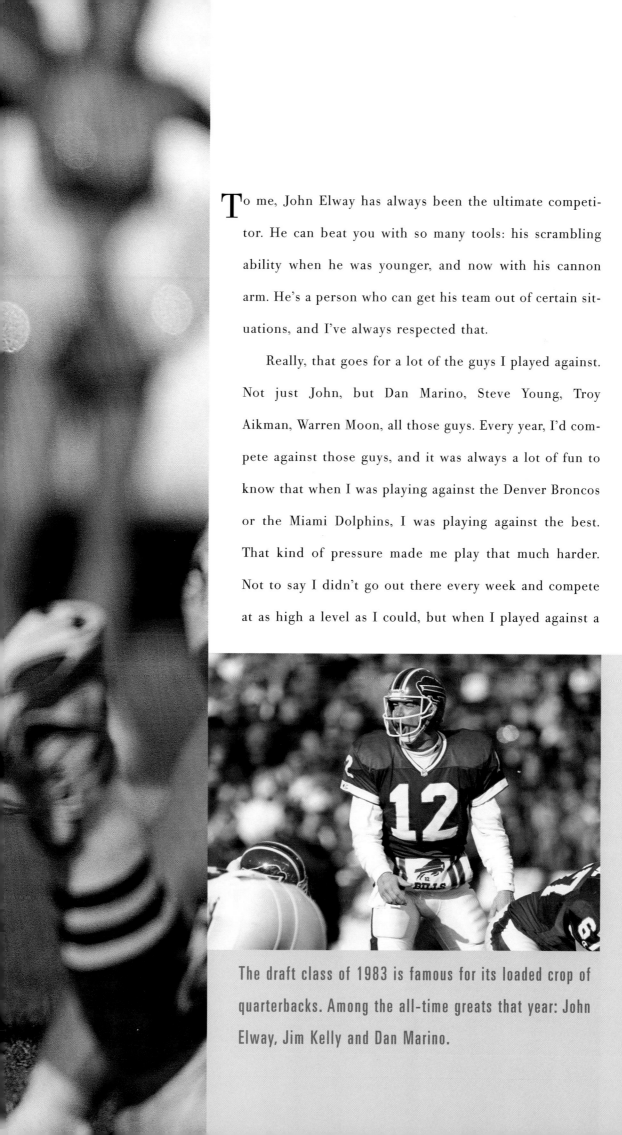

To me, John Elway has always been the ultimate competitor. He can beat you with so many tools: his scrambling ability when he was younger, and now with his cannon arm. He's a person who can get his team out of certain situations, and I've always respected that.

Really, that goes for a lot of the guys I played against. Not just John, but Dan Marino, Steve Young, Troy Aikman, Warren Moon, all those guys. Every year, I'd compete against those guys, and it was always a lot of fun to know that when I was playing against the Denver Broncos or the Miami Dolphins, I was playing against the best. That kind of pressure made me play that much harder. Not to say I didn't go out there every week and compete at as high a level as I could, but when I played against a

The draft class of 1983 is famous for its loaded crop of quarterbacks. Among the all-time greats that year: John Elway, Jim Kelly and Dan Marino.

guy like John Elway, I wanted to do well.

It definitely made me want to win more. I think John and I had a tremendous amount of respect for each other, but I don't know if you'd want to call it a rivalry. There were always rivalries between the teams, but I never went onto a football field saying, "OK, today I'm going to out-duel Dan Marino," or "Today, I'm going to throw for more touchdowns than John Elway."

A lot of people always wanted to say, "Here's a clash between the class of '83." Yes, on paper, that looks good and it's great publicity. But as far as individuals, from my own mind, I never went out there saying, "It's me competing against John today."

You always wanted to compete at a level so high that when the game was over, you knew that you left everything on the field. You

Adding to the woes of the class of 1983, Joe Montana alone
defeated Marino's Dolphins (in '84) and Elway's Broncos (in '89).

always want to feel proud of what you've accomplished, so when

you win, you win as a team. It was never me going out there and

saying, "We won the football game, but today I beat John Elway, or

Dan Marino." I've never looked at it that way because I respect

those guys too much, and they're close friends of mine. I'm sure

At times during his career, Elway's supporting cast left
him scrambling for cover. Not so in 1997, when he won
a Super Bowl in his fourth try.

they would probably say the same thing.

John and I are friends. I'm closer with Dan Marino than I am with John because I've seen Dan a lot more. But John and I are still friends. He has a busy schedule with so many things to do that, at times, it's tough to sit down and shoot the bull. But when we're at golf tournaments, we like to have a few beers together and chat. If I'm sitting there talking to John, there are probably 40 or 50 people around us. It's not always the easiest, but when all the quarterbacks get together at the Quarterback Challenge or a golf tournament, it's always nice to sit down and talk. I just remember how good of a golfer John is and how bad I am. John can kill the ball. He gets to play a lot. I don't get to play much golf (in Buffalo).

I spoke with John at the beginning of the season, and one of the questions I asked him was, "Why are you coming back? Is one of the reasons the team you have around you?" He said yes, absolutely.

It might be a different situation if he didn't have the cast of people that he has around him. There's no doubt that it weighed heavily on his decision. When you have an offensive system like Mike Shanahan has, a running back like Terrell Davis, a tight end like Shannon Sharpe, a receiver like Ed McCaffrey and a defense that can play,

Tony Eason struggled woefully in his one Super Bowl appearance, while Troy Aikman twice beat Kelly's Bills.

you'd almost be a fool not to come back.

If you feel you have the physical talent to do it, why not? Maybe if his team had lost a lot of people to free agency, or if his offensive linemen weren't going to be there, maybe that's a good reason to walk away. Then you can walk away from the game on top. But he knew he had a chance to repeat. He knew he could come back and win another Super Bowl. I know he hurt his hamstring during the (1998) season, but whether he's on the field or off the field, he's still the leader and the team captain. People are still looking to him for guidance.

When John won the Super Bowl, I couldn't have been any happier, finally getting that monkey off of the backs of all the members of the quarterback class of '83. But more importantly, a quarterback like John had been there three times and hadn't won one. Just like myself. I was there four times and didn't win one.

To get there means a lot, but to some people, if you don't win, you're not a true champion. But if you've ever been on a team, or if you've been a player, or even if you've been in competitive sports, you know what it's like to (play for a championship). Just to get there is saying a lot, but not everybody looks at it that way. I think those people who don't look at it that way have never played on a team. They've either never been in competitive sports, or they just don't like your team.

I knew whoever I was playing against from the class of '83, whether it was John or Dan, or guys like Ken O'Brien or Tony Eason, we were always going to battle. If you were ever up 21 points, you never felt comfortable until the game was over because you always knew who the quarterback was on the other team. With a guy like John Elway, the game was never over until there were all zeros shown on that clock.

Jim Kelly played two years in the USFL before coming to the NFL and joining the rest of the famous quarterback draft class of 1983: Tony Eason, Todd Blackledge, Ken O'Brien, Dan Marino and John Elway. Kelly retired in 1996 after an 11-year career with the Bills. In honor of their son, Hunter, Jim and his wife, Jill, have established Hunter's Hope, an organization designed to raise funds and awareness of Krabbe Disease and related disorders. Donations can be sent to Hunter's Hope; P.O. Box 643; Orchard Park, NY 14127; Phone: (716) 667-1200; Fax: (716) 667-1212; e-mail hunterhope@aol.com; http://members.aol.com/hunter-hope/main.html.

Agony to Ecstasy

9

"In all of the emotion (after the Super Bowl), I started thinking about how John and I had been through all of this together."

By Pat Bowlen

John Elway and I have been through a lot over the years. In fact, I don't think there's a quarterback and owner who have a closer relationship than the one I have with John. I don't think there probably ever will be again.

First it takes a unique situation. A lot of owners don't spend the time that I spend here at the facility with the players. And then there's free agency and other factors.

We've certainly been through a lot in the Super Bowl. In the first one (vs. the Giants in 1987), most of us were sort of mystified as to what it was all about. The AFC Championship Game in Cleveland was a long way from the hype and the intensity that surrounds the Super Bowl. It starts right from the night you win the AFC championship and really builds until the day you play the game two weeks later. All the attention and hype become overwhelming, especially when you get to the Super Bowl site.

We had a chance to be ahead, 17-9, against the Giants in the first half —

After losing to the 49ers in New Orleans, Broncos owner Pat Bowlen had just about decided that it wasn't worth winning the AFC title game if the team was going to lose in the Super Bowl.

a lot more, really. Maybe 21-7 or 28-7. From an offensive standpoint, it was a nightmare in the first half. We really had a chance to run away with the game.

John played well and it certainly wasn't his fault that we didn't win that game. I'm not going to place blame on anybody (for the 39-20 loss). But if I look back at the three Super Bowl losses, we had the best chance to win that game, by far. It's the one we should've won.

I was a lot more comfortable personally in Super Bowl XXII than I was in XXI because I knew the fire drill. So did John. I'm not saying Washington wasn't a better team or whatever and that the Redskins shouldn't have won. But Doug Williams passed for four touchdowns in the second quarter. Four touchdowns! It was unbelievable. They had us so confused on defense we didn't know what we were doing.

I had committed to do an interview at halftime and "listless" is not the word I'd use to describe how I felt. I mean, I know what they mean when they say "shell-shocked," in terms of wars and everything else. I was completely shell-shocked. Not only John, but also the whole team was shell-shocked (after the 42-10 defeat). The mental scars from those games will live with me for the rest of my life.

The third Super Bowl — the one against the 49ers (a 55-10 loss in XXIV) — well, we had all kinds of aspirations that we could beat the 49ers. And then . . . It's almost too painful to talk about.

I can remember seeing John an hour after the game. He was standing alone in the shower. That might have been a sadder moment for me than any

Elway stood tall in his first Super Bowl, throwing for 304 yards and one touchdown, but missed scoring chances eventually sacked the Broncos.

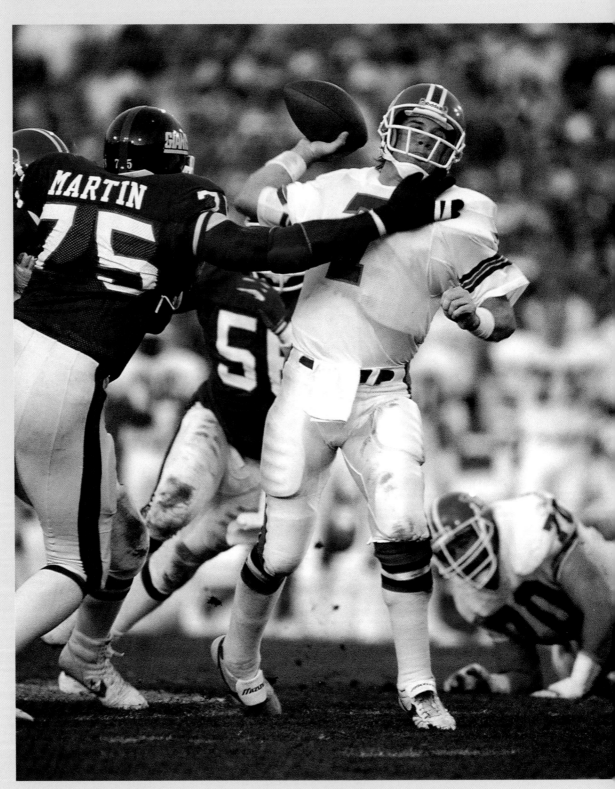

other time. It was a situation where I had sort of come to the conclusion — a day-dream kind of conclusion — that if I knew I was going to lose the Super Bowl, I didn't want to win the AFC Championship Game.

I remember saying that to Dan Reeves and him shaking his head and saying, "Well, you know, you can't look at it that way." But it was so painful for me, and I'm sure to some extent for John, that if somebody would have said you can go to the Super Bowl but you can't win, I wouldn't want to go again.

But by the time we got to San Diego (for Super Bowl XXXII vs. Green Bay) I was confident about our ability, and I didn't have the anxiety I'd had before. I'll give you one instance. I went out to practice on Wednesday of Super Bowl week. I usually stay for the whole practice during the playoffs, but after about 45 minutes, I said to myself, "You know, I don't care what anybody says. These guys are going to win." I could just tell by the attitude, by the approach, and by the intensity of the entire team.

It was clear Elway had a different attitude. The whole team was more confident, and it showed through John. On our first possession we scored a touchdown, which was important because the Packers had just scored. That showed me how intense Elway was, how determined he was for it to be different than in the '80s.

In the third quarter when he threw that interception (to Eugene Robinson), I was really mad. But I learned long ago to accept that as part of his game. He's aggressive and confident, and that showed on that play, even though it didn't work out. Later in the third quarter, I was worried that John had hurt himself when he dived into three defenders (on a key third-down conversion). I was worried he might fumble, too. But once again, it showed his determination. His emotion was such a big part of that game.

He'd waited so long. . . . Everyone who was pulling for him was emotional. And I think most of the country was pulling for him.

I had rehearsed my acceptance speech for the Super Bowl trophy three different times in the past, and I wasn't going to do it again. But in that game, when it became apparent we were going to win, I started thinking of what I wanted to say. You don't start thinking about speeches right after the moment of victory. It is a numbing, numbing moment. But in all the emotion, with all those feelings, I started thinking again about how John and I had been through all of this together. And as I thought about it, I realized it was clearly John's moment. It didn't matter who was MVP, or anything like that. I had to give John his due. It was his game. It will always be remembered as his game.

So I said, "John, this one's for you."

John has meant everything to me over the last 15 years. I've said it many times, and I'll say it again. I don't believe that I'll ever have another player like John Elway. I believe that he may have been the greatest player in the National Football League. I don't mind being tied in NFL history with John Elway. Not at all.

Broncos owner Pat Bowlen purchased the team in the spring of 1984, and that season second-year quarterback John Elway directed the squad to a 13-3 record and the AFC Western Division championship.

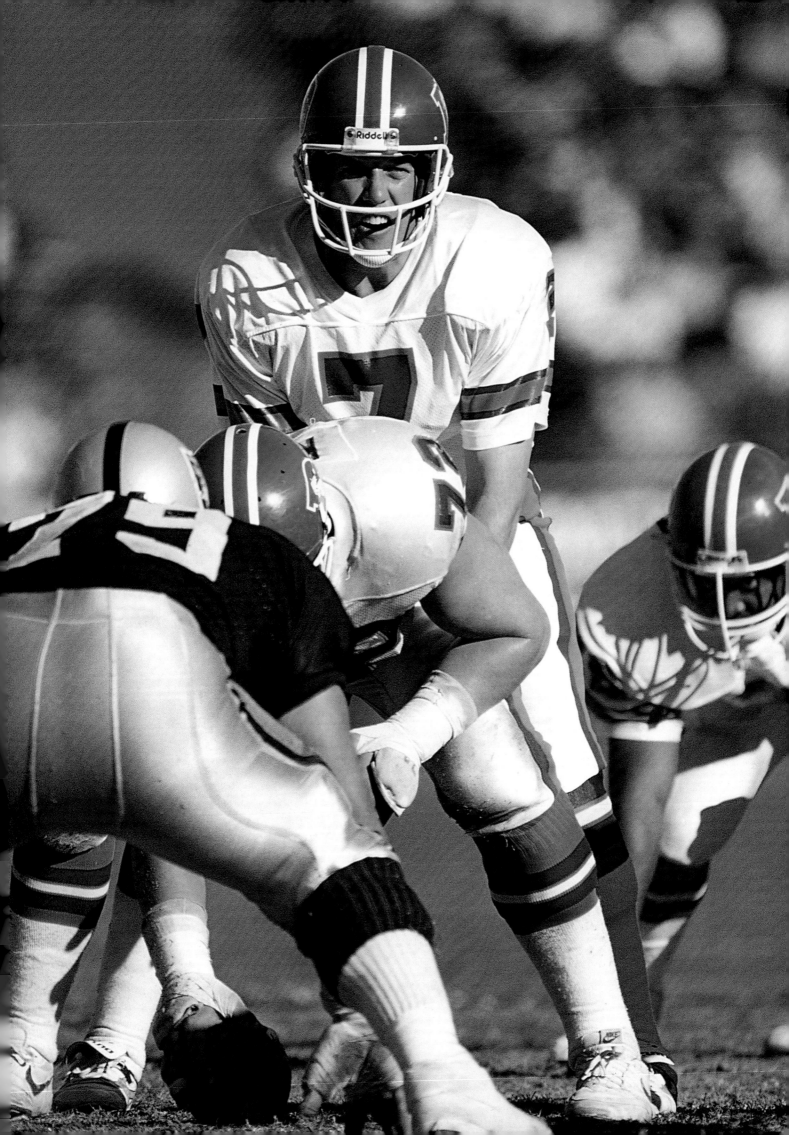

10

Field General

"John leads by example. He doesn't complain, even when he practically gets his head knocked off."

By Shannon Sharpe

As told to Clay Latimer

John Elway is one of the greatest leaders in the history of the sport. There's no doubt about that fact. And he leads in so many different ways.

I know as a receiver what I like most about John is that when you make a mistake he's not in your face. He doesn't try to bring attention to you. I've seen quarterbacks yelling and screaming and pointing at the guy (who makes a mistake), and I don't really think that is the right way to do it.

John has never done that to me or, for that matter, any other receiver that I can think of. Maybe once, you know, when we get behind closed doors he says, "This is what you should have done," or "What were you thinking when you ran this route?" But out there in public where everyone can see, that's not John.

I think that, in itself, is why everybody around here respects him so much. He could (point fingers) here and nothing would be said about it, but he won't. Sometimes you take things like that for granted. But as you get older and see how things unfold with other teams, you really have a greater appreciation of it.

John's leadership ability really surfaces on the comeback drives. He's so calm, he actually slows down. He's been in that situation so many times before. He knows he can do it. He knows it's just a matter of time, and he convinces us to believe we can do it, too. We believe we can go downfield and score because John will put the ball wherever it needs to be and he'll do whatever he needs to do. In fact, we know he's going to be even better when we have 90 yards to go with only a couple minutes left to play.

Here's a guy who owns all these records and is regarded as one of the greatest quarterbacks ever, yet he's able to turn it up a notch in desperate situations. That's what separates him from a lot of great quarterbacks. Time after time, he

finds a way to win against all the odds.

In the 1997 AFC Championship Game against the Steelers, we could see that we were starting to lose the momentum, that the tide was starting to turn in their favor. If they'd gotten the ball back, we weren't so sure we were going to be able to stop them. All of a sudden it's third down, and our coaching staff calls a play that wasn't in the game plan that week.

John says, "Run what you normally run if we run this play." But we weren't in the right (formation), so John simply says, "Well, go get open." I'm like, "You want me to run this, you want me to run that?" I remember telling myself to run six to eight yards and turn around. If he throws it, I figure, fine. If he doesn't throw it, I'll figure I read the wrong route. John put the ball in the only place it could have been thrown. The linebacker was in great position. I was very fortunate to come down with a catch. John stayed real cool. That's leadership.

Last year, when everything was going wrong, when we were being criticized and attacked in the media for being "just" 11-4 and then for the Bill Romanowski spitting incident, John decided to talk to the team.

Maybe some of us had started buying into it and listening to the media telling us we weren't that good. But here we were 11-4, and there were only a couple of teams that had better records. The guys are not accustomed to

Elway's leadership usually comes in the form of a few encouraging words, unlike some QBs who aren't afraid to make it known who ran the wrong route.

Through rain or sleet or snow, no NFL quarterback has delivered in more victories than John Elway.

having John stand up and talk, so once he said what he had to say, they knew it was in all sincerity.

It wasn't emotional. John wasn't pleading. He just talked in his normal tone. I remember him saying, "Hey, guys, this is what's going on, this is what we need to do. No one needs to panic. Let's just go and finish up the season strong and get ready for the playoffs. We're not as bad as anybody thinks we are. Remember how everybody was telling us how good we were when we were 6-0. Now all of a sudden we lost a couple games."

I felt that John's speech really brought us closer

together as a team because in all my years in Denver we'd never had a team meeting.

John leads by example. He doesn't complain, even when he practically gets his head knocked off. He doesn't ask for sympathy. He doesn't run off the field and have the cameras follow him to the sidelines and have everyone watch as the trainers and doctors look at him. He stays in there. He sucks it up and plays on. The guy is so tough. Here's a guy who has been sacked more than any other quarterback in the history of the game and has still passed for 50,000 career yards. That is just totally unheard of.

Quarterbacks get crushed. You always see them wearing flak jackets because of all the hits they take. Those hits add up, especially blind-side hits. And even when he throws the ball he can get knocked down. Those licks add up, too. If he's been sacked 500 times (actually 497 going into 1998), how many times has he been knocked down? At least double or triple that. At times there were some grimaces on his face when I knew he was feeling pretty bad. But he'd just call a play and go out and make a big play for us.

Basically, John Elway becomes a great leader just by being John Elway. He doesn't ask any more from his teammates than he is willing to give himself. I think that's the greatest form of leadership. You never doubt that he's going to put it on the line.

Shannon entered the league in 1990 as "Sterling's little brother" and now is regarded in a class by himself. The perennial Pro Bowl invitee has eclipsed 1,000 yards in receiving three times, tied for first all-time among tight ends.

Contributors

Photography by
Bob Rosato/Bob Rosato Sports Photography

Front cover photography by Walter Iooss

Additional photography by
Paul Chapman/BRSP
Jimmy Cribb/NFL Photos
Johnathan Daniel/Allsport USA
Tom DiPace
Tony Duffy/Allsport USA
Malcolm Emmons/NFL Photos
George Gojkovich/NFL Photos
Allen Kee/BRSP
Brad Mangin/Ron Vesely Photography
Ron Vesely
Allsport USA
NFL Photos

Writers
Clay Latimer, who interviewed Mike Shanahan, Terrell Davis,
Ed McCaffrey, Dan Reeves, Neil Smith, Pat Bowlen and Shannon Sharpe,
covers the NFL and the NBA for The Rocky Mountain News.

Pete Dougherty, who interviewed Brett Favre,
covers the Packers for the Green Bay Press-Gazette.

Ed Meyer, who interviewed Clay Matthews, writes for the Akron Beacon
Journal in Ohio and was the Browns' beat reporter from 1981 through 1994.

Tim O'Shei, who interviewed Jim Kelly,
is a freelance writer in the Buffalo area.